Congratulations!

Nothing compares to the feeling of loving and being loved.
If you have found my book, it means the true love and desire have come to light :)
Here you will find ideas that will inspire you to create a beautiful engagement moment for your beloved one.
Let's get started!

Make her feel *loved* and *appreciated*

1 Remember the place where you first met, go there and recreate the scene, tell her how special she is for you, the reasons why she is the love of your life and that she would make you the happiest man by saying Yes, I do! A bonus to your moment would be a congratulation message recorded before with the people she loves! The day/night can continue with a walk remembering your journey until this moment and promises for the new chapter!

◆ Don't forget to bring:
- her favorite flowers
- a drink that she likes
- a balloon and a pen, write a wish and let it fly away

Always be by her side

2. I am sure that she has a place from her bucket list that she would like to go. Now it's your chance to make her wish come true and organize a proposal plan. Search a beautiful place in that country/city (maybe a popular fountain, restaurant, one hill, the peace of a forest etc.) and create a long-lasting moment for the most beautiful I Do!

◆ Don't forget (depends on the place)
- to play your song
- order a cake that she likes
- write her a vow e-mail
- a balloon and a pen, write a wish and let it fly away
- enjoy every moment together

Love her every day a little bit more

3 How about a concert to an artist that she loves? You can pop up the question during the concert or maybe if you could talk before with the staff, they would help you go on stage and make a remarkable moment. Artists happily help create moments like this, you just have to send the right email so your plan can go as smooth as possible.

◆ Don't forget

- to talk with the staff
- scream how much you love her
- personalize the ring with a message like: you are my happy place!

Be her shoulder when she needs the most

4 If she loves the sea you can have *dinner on the beach* with candles, favorite food and dessert, playing your favorite song in the background and making her feel loved and appreciated. You can buy tickets for 2 days city break where you can enjoy and experience the new chapter of your life!

◆ **Don't forget**

- to buy all you need for dinner
- some lampion would be great
- a rose petal walkway if she loves the flowers

Make great *memories together*

5 *Write a huge message in the sand on the beach*: (marry me), rent a helicopter and show her what you just did :) Or maybe you have a hill in the area from where the message can be seen if you don't have from where to rent a helicopter. Or maybe you stay in a hotel on a hill and she will wake up called by you :) Adapt everything after the surroundings.

◆ Don't forget

- you can make her a seashell bouquet
- a good wine to celebrate
- the empty bottle of the wine you can use it for a message you both create it and keep as memory until you need to remember!

Make her days special

6 Go to the *adventure park* if your girl loves adrenaline:)

You can look for a good moment and ask her the big question for example like this:

"Throughout my life I was looking for my adventure partner and I found you. Nothing completes me more than you, no one knows me better than you, no one brings me the joy that you bring, so will you please be my adventure partner for the rest of our lives?"

◆ Don't forget
- safety first, bring a personalized helmet with Mrs.....
- joy and good mood

Love her imperfections

7 How about you ask her hand *on a plane*. Prepare yourselves a trip and just make sure you have arranged with the staff all the help that you need. Definitely SHE will always remember your gesture! Send an email to the air company you are flying with, see if involves any costs, and prepare to surprise her in applause of hundreds of people.

"From the moment I met you, I knew that I wanna fly next to you for the rest of my life and experience everything we can. You are amazing, kind and loving and I can't imagine my life without you. Will you please be my wife?

◆ **Don't forget**
- call the airline's center
- rehearse your love declaration

Make her compliments

8 If your girlfriend doesn't like crowds and she would like more of an intimate proposal, you can do it at your home. Decorate the room, cook/order something delicious, watch a movie together, preferable with love theme and when you're ready just pause the movie. "Having you here next to me it's the best feeling that I have ever experienced. With every passing day, i know that you are THE ONE, so please, will you marry me?"

◆ Don't forget

- create a cozy atmosphere
- rehearse your love declaration
- print some pictures with the most beautiful moments together

Try to understand her

9 Your girlfriend loves wine, and she is willing to try new experiences, then you should search near you a vineyard to organize a lunch table. You know what is her favorite meal, make sure that you have all you need there. Prepare in advance!
So, as a start to your moment, you can write a part of the message on a paper that can be delivered to her by the staff and the rest of the message you can complete with the proposal.

◆ Don't forget

- call and arrange the table
- be sure to have a great view
- rehearse the love declaration
- make sure that you are having a great time together

Learn to be a good listener, she will appreciate

10 Movie night at cinema can be a very good place to propose. You can make a small video with pictures of you two, insert also sentences with things that you love at her and surprise her happiness when you are together. Choose the right cinema, talk before with the staff so they let you play it on the screen and at the end of it you can ask the big question. I'm sure she will enjoy and always remember!

◆ Don't forget

- call and arrange with staff to play the video
- practice a love declaration
- invite friends to support you without her knowing

Love her for what she is

11 A walk in the forest can be transformed in a never forget proposal. Imagine yourself hearing the birds singing, the wind playing with leaves, you two having fun, and suddenly you find the perfect moment and spot for the big question! You can start your speech so: "All the peace that I feel today being here with you makes my heart melt. You complete me, you are the one that makes my universe stop and I would be more than happy if you will marry me."

◆ Don't forget

- the ring
- make sure to have a great view when you propose
- remember the place, so you can celebrate each year or when you go there
- enjoy every second

Hug her often

12 If she loves to be surrounded by friends and family, you can organize *a barbecue*, try not to tell someone because it's risky :). When you all sit down, ring the bell for a toast and feel free to express your feelings.

"Since I met you, my life has change in the best way possible, I love you more than I ever thought I could, you bring the color to my life. All of our loved ones are here witnessing the love and our moment, Will you marry me and spend the rest of your life with me?"

◆ Don't forget
- call everybody you know she loves
- make a list with all you need for the event
- make her feel the happiness of the moment

Travel as much as possible together

13 Imagine yourselves in *a hot air balloon*. One of the most popular destinations for this kind of activity is Cappadocia, Turkey! While exploring the world and enjoying the landscapes, I'm sure that this would be an awesome memory for your girlfriend! Living the dream of being together, you truly can say that love is in the air with an awesome YES!

◆ Don't forget
- to schedule the trip (the best months to go there is from April to May and September to October
- make a reservation to have also in the morning the view with hot air balloon
- the ring

Be present

14 A morning session of jogging can be relaxing and bracing, but when you will stop for an instant on a knee to ask her hand, that will become even more special. So, change the location where you can run, so she can admire also a new place, compose her a true love declaration and be prepared to impress her!

" I want all my mornings to start with you by my side, running through life together and having fun. You are my gift, my blessing, and just the thought that we can spend the life together makes my heart go crazy in the best way possible. Will you please be my wife?"

◆ Don't forget

- find a place with a view
- place safe the ring
- make her feel loved and appreciated

Enjoy every moment

15 Imagine yourselves having a picnic in a park early in the morning, watching the sunrise together, she in your arms, the food that you enjoy, all that can be a perfect moment to surprise her with the big question. Girls love the details and moments like this are hard to forget.

"Since I met you, my life changed in a way that I could never have imagined, I am happy, and I feel blessed. Mornings like this are simply rewarding and I would love that they became a habit next to you. So please, will you marry me?"

◆ Don't forget

- find a place from where you can enjoy the sunrise
- place safe the ring
- make her feel loved and appreciated

Be kind and loving

16 How about a karaoke night with your friends around, you're singing your favorite song and when you feel it's the right moment, just start improvising lyrics and make it sound special, as your moment! Make her feel loved and appreciated, look her in the eyes and tell her how much she means to you, music will help you express the feelings and also will relax the moment! You can also invite her to dance and at the end of the song pop up the big question:)

◆ Don't forget

- find a place you both like
- place safe the ring
- compose at home some lyrics that define you as a couple and reasons why she should say the big yes :)

Prepare a breakfast

17 If your girlfriend likes sometimes lazy mornings in the weekend, just you two, no phones to disturb you, the silence of home, then you should think to prepare her the breakfast that she will never forget. You can use toast bread to make letters with the text "will you marry me?" Arrange the table where you put also things that she loves to eat, some relaxing music in the background, a big bouquet of flowers, a good speech and you just created a perfect moment for your next big step!

◆ Don't forget
- be sure that no one will bother you
- she has nothing scheduled
- buy everything you need so you can enjoy the moment without stress

Be spontaneous

18 Your girlfriend loves football games, she has a favorite team and the crowds doesn't bother her when it comes to express the feelings? Then all you need to do is to get in touch with the staff of the stadium to see how you can pop up the question with the help of the big screen, to establish when it's the right moment for you to do that, buy a ring that represent her and prepare your voice because in that noise you will need to scream to be heard. Definitely she will never forget your proposal!

◆ Don't forget

- to have good seats for the big moment
- put safe the ring
- prepare your speech loud and clear

Surprise her often

19 Her birthday is coming, so you can arrange for her a surprise party. Invite all the people that she loves, maybe she has friends that she hasn't seen for a while, search a location that has a meaning for your relationship, you can create also a short video with pictures from your beginning as a couple, create a love declaration and be ready for the big question live:)
Make sure she feels all the love that you have for her and enjoy the moment together!

◆Don't forget

- book the place
- invite the loved ones
- make sure everyone knows that is a surprise party and they have to be very discrete

Communicate and listen

20 If your girlfriend loves to run, you could arrange a proposal at the finish line of a marathon. Take into account that you must run with her because it's easier when your loved one is by your side. So, make sure to put the ring in a safe place, have the best speech ever in your head, talk with someone to take some pictures with the moment and enjoy what comes. Surely, it will be a moment you will always remember! You can celebrate the double moment together: finishing the marathon and your engagement!

◆ Don't forget

- book for the race
- talk with the run photographer
- rehearse the love declaration for the best moment of your relationship

Create moments to remember

21 Dinner on a rooftop? Sure, that would be amazing. Imagine yourself a quiet evening, the stars shining, your favorite music in the background, a fluffy blanket on the floor, so you can watch the sky, her favorite food on the table, the best wine, all that can really make your moment magic. Make her feel appreciated, yeah :) everyone loves to hear good words and when they come from your future fiancé is a big plus.
In this kind of moments, you know that you have the right person next to you!

◆ **Don't forget**

- make a cozy atmosphere
- you can list some picture with you two from the beginning of your relationship
- buy everything you need for dinner
- the ring and words :)

Smile and enjoy

22 How about a professional photo shooting? Maybe she has a season that she loves or a favorite place, so, depending on what you decide, you will adapt your proposal. Let's say you will choose an autumn shoot, you can use leaves to write the biggest marry me and take the final pictures in that area. Make sure to have a good photographer that understands your requests and enjoy every picture!
You can also frame some pictures with your best moments and place them in the surroundings.

◆ Don't forget

- choose the best moment
- find a good photographer
- the ring and words :)
- a bottle of wine and two glasses to celebrate your moment

Enjoy the ride

23 How about a cruise proposal? You can arrange one week off to a favorite destination and enjoy every moment of it. Take into account that most of the cruise lines offer an engagement package. You will have the staff at your service to help you with your ideas, or if you need other suggestions they will be glad to help you. Imagine the view, the smell of the ocean and all the cruise services at your feet. Your fiancé will be thrilled. Love is awesome :)

◆ Don't forget

- choose the time of the year
- book the cruise
- check the schedule of your girlfriend
- relax and make some beautiful memories

Live, love, repeat

24 Pop-up the question in a hotel can also be a good idea. Around the world, you can find hotels that have had included proposal packages. To make your moment even more romantic, try to find a hotel that has a fantastic view. Imagine seeing from your window views like: a lake, mountains, sea, castle, volcano, northern lights (aurora borealis), a vineyard, air balloons flying, waterfall, lavender field, etc.
Choose what it's best for you and go to an amazing life trip next to your future wife. Half of our work will be done by the surroundings! :)

◆ Don't forget

- choose the time of the year taking into consideration what do you want to experience from the list above
- book everything and imagine the right moment

25 Writing can be very helpful. If you love to write, you can make a small journal of your relationship, where you can describe the beautiful moments spend together, all the feelings, what does she mean to you, the places that you visit together, how she changed your life, the parties that you've been together, friends that you have, pictures that you love and in the end the plans that you have made for your future and that you would be thrilled if she accepts to be your wife. She will be amazed, having written the "radiography" of your relationship. Then invite her in a peaceful place to hand her the big present and ask her the big question!

◆ Don't forget

- sincerely write all that you feel and wish for
- find a good place for the magic moment
- place the ring at the end of the book

26 How about a treasure hunt proposal?! All the clues that she has to find out are details about: the place where you first met, the country that she would like to visit, maybe she has preference about the names of your future children :), food that she likes to eat, things that she hates, the place where you first kissed, the movie that you like, the first I love you, etc.

At the end of the game, the last clue should be about the big question: "Two people are stronger together, but her answer is the key for the journey"

Here is everybody ready and you on your knee asking her loud and clearly: will you marry me? Good luck!

◆ Don't forget

- *find the right spot for this adventure*
- *call your friends to help*
- *make the game fun, enjoyable putting you and your relationship in the center of it*

Validate her emotions

27 How about the game hide and seek?! You can use paint that glows in the dark, write on a wall the magic sentence, and hide yourself in the room that has the message. Don't forget to play one time just for fun and then you can apply what I said above.
Let her enjoy every moment with you, to rediscover the beauty of playing and having fun together!
After she discovers the message, make sure you have the ring prepared, a good wine to celebrate and perhaps two t - shirt with "Freshly engaged" message!

◆ Don't forget

- *test one night before to be sure that your message it's visible and clear*
- *have the ring in your pocket*
- *wine in the fridge*
- *be happy*

Make memories together

28 5,4,3,2,1 happy new year :)
How about a proposal during New Year's Eve?! Finishing the year as boyfriend and girlfriend and starting the new year engaged. That sounds more than great. So, maybe you are at a party, or you have invited some friends to your place, or it's just the two of you, in every case you can propose after the final counting: "Will you marry me" will be a double happiness and the best memory each new year. The excitement of the new beginning together celebrated with beautiful fireworks. Enjoy it all!

◆ Don't forget

- the ring in a safe place
- a good champagne
- good mood, nothing in your way that can ruin the moment
- a close and safe spot for the fireworks view

Made every day count

29 Earlier in this book, I said that you can propose in an airplane. But you can also propose in an airport! Imagine your girlfriend in a business trip for 2 weeks, you miss her deeply, and you feel that your moment is here. So, grab a couple of friends, make together a sign with the magic question, maybe you have a friend that can sing your song in the background, talk with the airport security about your plan, so they can support you, buy a nice bouquet of her favorite flowers and wait to her with open arms and a happy heart. I'm sure she will be thrilled becoming your wife.

◆ Don't forget

- make the question really visible
- talk with the friends that are discrete to not uncover your moment
- the ring, the flowers and music if the airport security accepts!

Be the best friend of each other

30 How about propose travelling by train. Maybe near you there is a historical line like the steam locomotive, known not for the speed but more for relax where you can enjoy the surroundings, the view, without being next to the people in a rush. If you love to travel you can find this kind of train in Europe in countries like: Germany, Romania, Scotland, Austria. I'm sure that she would enjoy this kind of proposal. Before you pop up the question, depending on which line you choose to travel with, maybe you find a love story, that you can connect to your story finishing with the magic question. A local guide could help you!

◆ **Don't forget**

- *find a local guide for the story*
- *put the ring in a safe place*
- *talk with the train staff about your plans*
- *enjoy the ride, so she can have the same good energy*

Laugh every day together

31 Hmm, how about a proposal during the Christmas tree decorations?! The special moment of preparing the house for the big holiday can be joyful and perfectly placed for a happy memory. You can order or do it yourself a small decoration for the tree with the big question, rehearse a nice speech about all the moments you share together so far and why would you love that she became your wife. Appreciate all the things that she have done for you and make sure she feels all the love that you have for her. From time to time, the people we love must know how much they mean to us.

◆ **Don't forget**

- *make the special ornament*
- *the ring and the speech*
- *a good wine or what she loves to drink*
- *a holiday atmosphere*

A video to remember...

32 Start collecting all the memories that you have together: pictures, short videos, love messages, presents etc. and start selecting what it's more suggestive for your relationship. After you have all prepared, record a message where you tell her everything she means to you, the reason why you choose her to be your half etc. Put all the stuff together, edit to the latest detail. Then invite her in a place where you can enjoy the video on a big screen, and in the end you can ask her in real life the big question. Choosing this type of proposal can remind her of your special moments together and the growth of your relationship.

◆ **Don't forget**

- *find the place to watch the video*
- *the ring and the final speech*
- *a cozy atmosphere*
- *invite people that she loves if it's a public space*

A sunrise to remember...

33 I'm sure that you can find a perfect spot near you or outside your comfort zone from where you can see the best sunrise ever next to your love. You can tell her that you will enjoy nature together, and you will stay overnight in a tent enjoying some marshmallow, watching stars, remembering your start as a couple or something that you know she likes to talk about.

Early in the morning, before you wake her up, be sure that you know where is the best spot to see the sunrise, prepare your speech in mind, the ring and a big smile on your face. Let her feel comfortable as possible, so she can enjoy every piece of every moment together. These are the best memories

◆ **Don't forget**

- *find the place*
- *the ring and the final speech*
- *a cozy atmosphere*
- *make pictures before and after*

Enjoy a good catch together

34 If you and your girlfriend love going *fishing together*, you have the perfect place where to propose. So you already have a lake or a sea, choose if you are going alone, or you consider that you want your friends to be there too, engrave a message on a small metal plate that can be attached to her hook: "you are my best catch, I love you!" make sure she sees the message on the right moment and surprise her with the best love declaration ever. Having things in common is awesome and when you connect them to the heart everything becomes unforgettable. Laugh a lot, capture the moment and enjoy every breath together.

◆ **Don't forget**

- *find the place*
- *talk with friends if you decide to go with them also*
- *a cozy atmosphere*
- *the ring and the speech*

Adventure, fresh air and good memories

35 If you enjoy walking in the nature, how about a hiking proposal?! Going together through the mountains in the adventure of your lives. As soon as you have the location you can start thinking to the moment of the day: early in the morning to catch the sunrise, at the end of the day to catch the sunset, or you just let yourself on a wave considering that when you feel the moment you will stop there for the proposal. The benefits of hiking is that you have almost in every corner of the nature something awesome to enjoy: different sounds, fascinating views, fresh air, good vibe etc. If you are going alone, make sure that you place the camera in a good spot to capture the moment.

◆ **Don't forget**

- *find the place*
- *talk with friends if you decide to go with them also*
- *the ring*

Love is all that matters

At the end of this chapters, maybe you have questions or doubts about the moment. Stop for a second and think about the person you have next to you and if you feel that the person next to you is the one then it's worth going forward for greater moments as a couple. In love, like in life, we all have ups and downs, but in the end all that matters is love and knowing that you can count on each other no matter what, trust me, really is the best feeling! Learn to apologize, accept that life is not always pink, and make great memories together. I hope that you will find in this book a good idea for your special moment. If not, maybe you find inspiration for other beautiful moments together. Hugs and kisses!

◆ Don't forget

- *Life is great when you have the right person beside you!*